OUTSIDE THE CAVE

GEORGIA S. McDADE

Cover Art © Adam Korpak

Book & Cover Design by Vladimir Verano, Third Place Press

Contact the author:

gsmcdade@msn.com

SECOND EDITION

ISBN: 978-0-9967010-0-6

 PRINTED BY THIRD PLACE PRESS
Lake Forest Park, Washington
press@thirdplacebooks.com

This book is dedicated to anyone who wants to learn. There is so much to be learned—what to do, what not to do. Quite often when we are privy to what someone else has learned, we can escape some of the many pitfalls which fill life. By no means have I always observed or observed correctly, but I have always wanted to help others avoid as many pitfalls as possible.

ACKNOWLEDGEMENTS

Thanks to Susan Platt, Ph. D., who introduced me to George Brandt, owner of Gallery 110 in Seattle, Washington.

It was Susan who suggested George invite the African-American Writers' Alliance to write about works of artists showcased in the Gallery. As a result I wrote more regularly than ever before—about the artists' works and about subjects I had planned to write about or begun to write about years earlier.

I thank the writers in the Alliance, who, without ever telling me to write poetry rather than stories, encouraged and nourished me as I penned more and more poems.

I thank the visual artists Betsy Best-Spadaro, Elizabeth Halfacre, Pamela Mills, Adam Korpak, John Martinotti, Karen Kosoglad, Cindy Hall, and David Traylor for works that inspired me.

Thanks to family, friends, and students who read or listened to the poetry and encouraged me. They and audience members who spoke with me about a poem, requested that I read a poem, or asked for a copy of a poem inspired me to produce this collection.

Thanks to computer genius Paul Nichols for being the great teacher he is.

CONTENTS

DECLARATIONS

INTRODUCTION

One wants a Teller in a time like this. ~ Gwendolyn Brooks

OUTSIDE THE CAVE is grounded in the author's memory and gift for weaving the past with the present. Woven throughout her scores of poems are metaphors, ironies, and paradoxes of living and surviving in challenging times. In its four sections—Exclamations, Interrogatives, Imperatives, and Declarations—"Lives are punctuated by revelations and epiphanies" connects the poems. Within these lives are male and female angst, amorphous questions about death, war condemnation, life queries, and omniscience awareness. Exhibiting emotional stability, persons in her poems sometimes sacrifice their yearnings, even their selfness in order to avert conundrums. Women occasionally become like Zora Neale Hurston's "mules of the world." They may be "Embarrassed" when lovers and spouses mentally or physically cheat. In "No Way—at Least Not Tonight," a woman would rather risk another beating, even her life, than to conceive another child with a drunk and abusive husband. Men too often feel "all occasions do inform against" them, so they fight battles often initiated or created by others or respond to what they believe is their responsibility. "The Contractor" viewed both sides of such a dilemma. McDade's concerns run a gamut: couples and children, joys and sorrows, belief and unbelief. Rather than conceiving children out of love and understanding, for example, a couple in "Let's Get Naked" shed clothes only for sexual gratification.

When a child results, McDade challenges readers to consider disappointment in the voices of children who feel "Abandoned." More stable couples frequently divorce, the consequence being a child with "two houses, two toothbrushes, two Thanksgivings…" in "Two for One," a child striving for steadiness and in thoughts only expressing suppressed desires, wishing for parent reconciliation and thus one home.

Sacrifices originate from other sources. There's a timely war poem, "Folded Flag," a dead father plus family and friends who suffer the heaviness of death and a collapsed future. In addition, "Precious Cargo" is a misnomer for dead veterans. They are not goods, freight, or a shipment; they are instead fellow individuals, body, mind, and soul missed by loved ones. The end of a familiar peace comes with unexpected death; in "Mad at God" a person vacillates between blasphemy and forgiveness despite the many condolences.

Balancing these punctuated lives are additional threads or "imperatives" in several poems. The author tells readers to "juggle on," life is full of unavoidable rhythms. Ironically, life can be fortuitous. In "If Only" persons who wish for a conflict-free life may find that it ends in no life. Preparing for living occasionally begins "When Sunday Comes." For many who believe, Omniscience reigns, heals, and provides comfort for the unwanted challenges of Monday through Saturday and Sunday too. Always are stories told, testimonies given. When a miracle or an epiphany radiates from the soul always are some who "join in the spontaneity without understanding" "Why Some of Us Holler."

As Margaret Walker says in "For My People," there is strength and healing pulsing in our spirits. This spirit pulses in these poems too as the author retells her stories and observations about the challenges and joys of living daily outside the cave. I am honored to read Dr. Georgia S. McDade's first edition of OUTSIDE THE CAVE.

Minnie A. Collins,
Emeritus English Faculty,
Seattle Central Community College
November 2008

EXCLAMATIONS

After the Fact

It's stunning.
It's baffling.
It's so unbelievable.
It's overwhelming.
No one saw it coming.
No one has an answer.
Not mother or brother, sister or father.
Not friends nor co-workers.
The computer has no clues.
And yet it happened.
In all of its horridness.

When are we survivors going to learn?
There's little we can do about the fact.
But there's much we can do after the fact.
Each of us can choose, decide.
Each of us can give whatever it is we think may have made
a difference, perhaps prevent a repeat of the fact.

03/29/06

Anatomy

This nose.

These arms.

This shape.

And please add this size, these lips.

And, Lord, remember this hair!

Instead of a plain thank you, listeners got some black anatomy.

I know exactly what she meant and means.

I wonder how many others did and do.

03/06/07

Bring 'Em On

The President says he's grateful to the soldiers who have lost their lives.

He says he "mourned every loss."

He says he "honored every name."

I shouldn't not believe him because he sends more troops on more trips.

He may be the only person who thinks his mission is accomplished.

I can't get past his "Bring 'em on."

I don't know what he meant.

I still don't know what he expected when he said that.

Did he think the terrorists would not hear him?

Or did he think they would dismiss him?

Perhaps he thought the tough cowboy talk would scare them.

I wonder if the President knows there are those who

consider him a terrorist, the leader of the terrorists.

2004

Danger

What part of danger don't you understand?
Timber!
Five-Alarm Fire!
Category 5 Hurricane!
Fox in henhouse!
8.5 on the Richter Scale!
Canaries dropping in a coal mine!
How many ways can I say danger?
 I'm saying it every way I can!
There is danger.
And, yet, no one hears me.

02/22/05

Embarrassed

With a sneer of his lips and disgust in his eyes, he said,

I am embarrassed that they lie.

I am embarrassed that they cheat.

I am embarrassed that they steal.

I am embarrassed that they hurt.

I am embarrassed that they abuse.

I am embarrassed that they misuse.

I am embarrassed that they deceive.

I am embarrassed that they kill.

But it's not just black people that I am embarrassed for.

I am embarrassed for white people too.

I am embarrassed that they lie.

I am embarrassed that they cheat.

I am embarrassed that they steal.

I am embarrassed that they hurt.

I am embarrassed that they abuse.

I am embarrassed that they misuse.

I am embarrassed that they deceive.

I am embarrassed that they kill.

She couldn't, wouldn't disagree with him. She wanted people—black and white—to do better, to be better. But she knew her greatest success most likely would be with herself. And she didn't dare tell him how embarrassed she was that after all these years she was still suffering his lying, cheating, hurting, abusing, misusing, deceiving, and killing—her. This was something he could stop. And she wanted so badly for it to stop. But she was embarrassed to tell him, much too embarrassed.

06/92

God and His Rules

God has to change the rules—again.

Really.

If He does not want to be lonely in heaven, He must change the
rules.

He did it for Noah's generation: He began again.

He did it for us: without shedding of blood—the blood of Jesus—is no remission
of sins.

So, God has to change the rules—again.

If He doesn't, He may be as lonely in Heaven as James Weldon Johnson said God
was lonely at creation.

Ok, many of us do SOME of what He tells us to do, and others of us don't do
SOME of what He tells us not to do.

And some of us do and don't do SOME of both.

But nobody I know does and doesn't do everything we are commanded to do and
not do.

Some of us try—sometime.

We walk around as if each of us has a special Bible.

One woman admitted to the seminary teacher, "I never read the Bible without
whiteout."

Everybody was amazed.

The young woman explained, "When I disagree with something, I just cross it out."

People laughed; I did too.

But the more I think about it, the more I think most of us—to be honest—need
to confess: we too carry whiteout—the invisible kind; we don't literally
white out what we don't agree with.

But we eliminate some of those rules, rationalize and justify not following others.

So, in this test of life we may do very well in this section or several sections, but
we fail miserably in another section.

Telling us to let him who is without sin cast the first stone is hilarious—unless
     He does not want any stones cast.
And maybe that's it.
Maybe He wants no stones cast.
Maybe He wants us to go around building, tearing down only that which is bad.
Do you think?
I still think God may be lonely in heaven.
We just have so much to do and not do.
We may not commit the sin, but we fail to stop the sin when we can.
Most of us do nothing, would never do anything to be incarcerated by the state.
But if God physically incarcerated, we would be in jail.
And my pastor friend says if the police came and arrested everyone in church
     for being a Christian, authorities would have to let us go because there
     is not enough evidence to convict us.
God would incarcerate us for breaking rules; man would let us go for not
     keeping the rules.
The possibility exists that God may be lonely in heaven if He does not change
     the rules—again.

09/05/04

He Did Not Tell Us

Told everybody he was dying—
Everybody but his family!
 Well, ok, forget the hyperbole. He did not tell e v e r y b o d y!
But he told quite a few people!
Said there was nothing to be done.
Said he did not want to worry us.
All we can do is speculate:
Did he think we were too weak?
Maybe we were. Maybe we are.
But he didn't know!
Maybe we weren't.
But maybe we were.
Maybe we're like tea bags.
You can't tell how strong we are until we're in hot water!
And his leaving would definitely require our being strong.
Not to give us one more kiss.
Not to give us one more hug.
How could he deny us one more I love you?
We could have thanked him one more time.
We never imagined life without him.
Saying bye would have been hard,
But no one can convince me that this is not harder.
Maybe we needed to say, "I'm sorry" one more time.
Maybe we needed to forgive or be forgiven.
Maybe we needed to apologize or be apologized to.
We could have said "I love you" one more time.
We could have said goodbye.
Saying it, knowing it was our last would have been so hard.

But this is harder.

We don't doubt his decision.

We know he cared.

We know he loved us.

Now we do less that requires an "I'm sorry."

We argue less about who was wrong.

And we say "I'm sorry" more easily.

Sometimes we apologize only to be asked, "Why are you apologizing?"

We say "I love you" more often.

We do not wait for holidays to get together or give a gift.

We say "Bye" knowing this may be the last "Bye."

He's gone; we hurt.

But he taught us even in his passing.

Knowing he is "pain-free," "in a better place,"

      "gone to be home with God" does not help us, at least not for long.

But we are forever grateful that we had him in our lives.

Still, we wish he had not chosen not to tell us.

2004

To Quit or To Quit

He said he'd love her when she quit.

She said she'd quit when he loved her.

So the two of them went round and round over and over.

Both of them made demands.

Was either's demands outlandish?

Does love require we quit what we love?

Only when the habit is bad or unhealthy?

Can it?

Should it?

Who knows?

All I know is he said, "If you love me, you'll
       quit that" and she said, "If you love me, I'll quit
       that."

And they didn't go anywhere 'cause she wouldn't quit 'till
       he loved her and he wouldn't love her 'till she quit.

08/03/04

The Little Troopers

The Little Troopers are something!

They are awakened at 5:30 a.m. five days a week.

By 6:45 a. m. they are at the daycare center.

They eat.

Two go to school.

One stays with the ladies at daycare.

(The Little People correct anyone who fails to distinguish
daycare from school.)

They know someone will pick them up.

They don't know who.

They don't know when.

Yet someone shows.

The smaller two greet with hugs any sane person wants to get.

They are admirable, the little trio.

They are the most adapting people I know, ambiguity and
contradictions notwithstanding.

They know rules at Mom's place which is someone else's place.

They know rules at the homes of their dad.

But they know the rules at the homes of their grandma,
maternal grandma and stepgrandpa,
paternal grandpa and stepgrandma, two aunts, and
an uncle, several great aunts—all family, family
whose only element of unity is the little troopers.

They know the meaning of diversity but don't know they know.

They know the different foods in the different houses.

They know the different bedtimes.

They know who's strict and who's lax.

They know what to say to whom when and how.

They know all kinds of music.

They know they always go to church when they stay at some places.

They know they never go to church when they stay at other

        places, remember someone told them, "I don't go to nobody's church!"

They don't know that most people spend most weekends at home.

They've been away from home as many as twelve consecutive weekends....

On my best days, I say,

"They are learning so much about differences so early!"

"The resiliency outweighs the vulnerability," I say.

"This is good," I say.

"They will be able to adapt," I say.

"They'll be tolerant," I say.

But then I ask, "Where are you going this weekend?"

The little talker says, "I have no idea," or "I don't have a clue."

And then as I hope I can get them this weekend, I say to myself,

        "I wish they could sleep 'til seven."

And then I say, "NO! I'll let them sleep until they awake."

02/05

Somebody's Dreams

There's no sign of the countless photographs.

There are mud-laden jars of home-canned fruit.

There's a used-to-be fabulous house where no one can live.

There's a luxury-loaded car no one can drive.

Furniture fit for a castle is parked along what used to be roads.

Absolutely nothing says there was a garden here or there
        was one here over forty years.

The lavish, one-of-a-kind, heirloom Mardi Gras costumes
        are gone with the wind and rain.

And though there's no place to look for help, opportunities abound to give
        help.

And here on the ground, actually in trees and on rooftops
        too are remnants of somebody's dreams.

02/07

INTERROGATIVES

At This Time

I know He's here.

He's everywhere.

I know He knows.

He knows everything.

I know He can.

He has all power.

He hears, sees, touches, tastes, smells all things.

I know He does.

What I want to know is why He does.

04/12/06

Decisions: One Person's View

"How do you spray a person from close range?" asked the soldier.

"The same way you spray a person from long range," said the lady.

"Actually, close range is easier.

There's no missing.

You get a wasted person but no wasted bullets."

Granted, there may be a problem with the initial spray,

       most likely a problem with the first shot.

But once past the initial firing, subsequent firings become easier.

Why?

Simple.

After guessing about the approaching person, this one aims

       no harm and that one means harm and being wrong

       once or twice—or several times—then you shoot first.

Now, you may ask questions later.

You may be reprimanded.

But the enemy—and sometimes a fellow soldier—will be dead.

And that's one fewer person—oops—enemy to wonder about.

How do you spray a person from close range?

10/12/04

Folded Flag

Look at the little fellow.

He holds the flag proudly.

Mom instructed him to stand tall, stand straight.

Just as Grandma had instructed Dad and Greatgrandma
  had instructed Grandpa.

Holding the folded flag is an even greater task.

But Mom assured him he could do it.

And the little fellow wanted to do his part.

Mom wanted him to do his part.

She had reluctantly agreed Dad should do his part, do his duty
  for God, country, and family.

But Mom nor Dad never admitted Mom and Son would be
  here because Dad did his part.

The flag is heavy, especially the folded flag, and especially
  for such a little boy.

But somehow, somewhere, sometime, someone has always
  been willing to hold up a flag.

Just as somehow, somewhere, sometime, someone has always
  held up the folded flag.

Freedom is not free.

And few argue that it is.

But does it have to cost as much as it does?

08/03/04   Inspired by John Martinotti's photograph *Fallen Comrade*

Horrors

It's not as if I don't think about the slave castles and the
    Middle Passage and slavery in these United States of America.
I do.
I think about many other horrors: Holocaust, Hiroshima,
    Nagasaki, all those soldiers on all those beaches not
    playing parts in Spielberg movies.
I think about Salem witches, John Brown, Emmett Till,
    Medgar Evers, John F. Kennedy, MLK, RFK, Berlin,
    the Smith boys, the five Yates kids.
And now I think about New York which had never been on
    my list of horrors.
Now I see planes, but they are missiles or bombs.
Now I see running people, but no joggers they.
They are running for a different reason.
I see fire, but it is billowing from the Towers.
I see smoke and ash, but neither comes from cigarettes.
I see steel but not raising skyscrapers; it is taking its own
    form, doing exactly what the strength of material
    textbooks say it will do, doing exactly what engineers know it will do.
I see bodies falling through the air but not immeasurable
    heights and without trampolines beneath them.
I see bodies pressed against windows but not the subway windows.
Graham Green's "Destruction is, after all, a form of
    creation" notwithstanding, how could anyone have
    thought the world needed another manmade horror?

2001

Ignorance

He didn't know Schwerner!

He did not know Schwerner.

An educated, well-traveled black man, and he didn't know Schwerner.

A few days later a ticket operator didn't know Emmett Till,
>   asked how to spell "her" name.

Reminds me of the college student who said he was six
>   when Dr. Martin Luther King, Jr., died so why
>   should he know anything about him.

Of course, this student couldn't say how old he was when
>   Columbus supposedly discovered America.

I tried to be calm; in each instance I tried.

I know. I know.

Nobody knows everything.

But not to know Schwerner, Goodman, and Cheney and Emmett Till....

At least I can rage on a page.

And I am raging, raging still.

So many unknown persons are dead, dead, dead because
>   some white folks thought black folks should not
>   vote, go to school, earn a livable wage, live.

I guess it is up to me to keep the memories alive.

I'm teaching as much as fast as often as I can.

Somebody's got to erase the ignorance.

Not for pain or vengeance but for pride and bravery,
>   gratitude with an uppercase G.

Who'll tell the stories?

03/05/06

Tired

I'm tired.

And like Fannie Lou Hamer, "I'm sick and tired of being sick and tired."

Oh, don't misunderstand.

This tiredness Geritol won't cure.

The tiredness comes not from what I eat or don't eat.

It can't be alleviated by sleeping.

Fresh air doesn't make it go away.

NO amount of money can eradicate it.

I'm tired of the high cost of living.

I'm tired of rampant unfairness, unequal opportunity,

limited access, no access.

Why can't today be the day that I and so many others like

me be refreshed?

05/26-27/00

Social Revolutions

Natural revolutions such as earthquakes, tsunamis, hurricanes, tornadoes,
>   volcanoes we can often escape IF we see them and know they are coming.
Social revolutions, however, rarely provide such escapes.
People-made revolutions we often don't see and fail to see coming.
Many of us say we want change, but not CHANGE.
Many of us want integration, but not INTEGRATION.
Many of us want affirmative action but not AFFIRMATIVE ACTION.
Many of us want diversity, but not DIVERSITY.
Many of us want equal rights, but not EQUAL RIGHTS.
Nobody wants to give up power regardless of how ill-gotten or how injurious to
>   the powerless.
Saying we intend to make a situation better for others never entails making our
>   situation worse.
Inevitably we encounter unintended consequences—something costs more, takes
>   longer.
So we institute policies and invent tools which supposedly remedy what the
>   revolution wrought.
We coin words to name what we do.
Much of the time we disdain the challenge of the new and go for the comfort of
>   the old.
The familiar is always an easier route or appears to be.
But the revolutions don't stop.
What we can do is attempt to minimize the negative unintended consequences.

07/14-15/06

Why?

A civic association
A nursing home
Post offices
Other workplaces
College campuses
High school campuses
McDonald's
Houses that somehow missed or stopped being homes

All settings for mass killings, some more than others.
Victims random sometimes, family and friends other times.
Not one perpetrator suffered an unheard of once-in-a-lifetime ailment.
Rejection, frustration, disappointment, loss, stress—all of us humans who live a
      while experience such to varying degrees.
Envy, jealousy, pain, failure, loneliness—all of us experience these too.
Yet no one can explain why some of us respond by hurting others and/or self and
      some of us respond by being kinder and/or gentler.

Was it post-traumatic stress?
Was there an accumulation of molehills?
Was there one mountain too many?
Was there no preparation for disaster?
Was it overwhelming tiredness?
Was it something added or subtracted,
      too little or too much?
Was there something someone could have done?

04/06/09

IMPERATIVES

A Balancing Act

Life's a balancing act.

You have to say some persons have to balance more than others.

Why may as well be immaterial.

You choose, make poor or incorrect choices, but not necessarily so.

You have responsibilities.

You have responsibilities thrust upon you.

To stay alive—and that's usually what's important—you juggle.

It seems anybody good at anything has to juggle.

Move to the left.

Move to the right.

Stand in the center.

Jump up.

Reach.

Reach farther.

Be still.

Don't you have to look before you leap?

But hesitate—and you may be lost.

Never be in any one position too long.

But what's too long?

Maybe Someone knows, but you probably don't, halo or not.

Continue the balancing act.

Just juggle on.

09/18/04   Inspired by Betsy Best-Spadaro's painting *Circus Mom XII*

Crowds

Beware the crowd.
Please beware the crowd.
You can't count on the crowd.
The crowd has a long history of fickleness.
The crowd supported the oration of Brutus—
Until Antony delivered his opposing view and got
the crowd's nod.
The crowd chose Barrabas, a criminal with a long record
Over Jesus Who had a record of helping and healing,
raising the dead even.
The crowd yelled "Hosanna" to this same Jesus one day
And "Crucify Him" one week later.
Please beware the crowd.
The crowd can get you killed more quickly than it can move
to another witless victim.
Again I say beware the crowd.

03/30/06

A Little Bit of Information

Once again I have to hear about
      another little black girl
      telling another little tale or
      presenting another little poem or
      singing another little song or
      reciting another little rap
      about other little black girls who call her white and
      little white girls who call her black.

How long has this been going on?
How long will it go on?
I have a feeling the answer is forever, the twelfth of never if
      you want to be specific.
Let them talk: You are what you are. You don't plan to
      change for them.
Little black girl, define yourself!
Defining yourself is your best defense.
Ignore little black girls and little white girls who think they
      can define you.
Life really is short, much too short you'll realize as you age.
Much too much is happening for you to spend your time
      trying to get little black girls and little white girls
      to recognize and accept your genuine brand of blackness.
And do be genuine, little black girl.

And, little black girl, remember this information as
        throughout your life you encounter
        other little black boys and little white boys, little
        white men and little white women, little black
        women and little black men.
Your sanity and your life may be saved with this
        little bit of information.

05/15/06

No Apologies Please

I'm sorry.

I apologize.

Please accept my apology.

I made a mistake.

I accept the responsibility.

I did not mean it.

Please.

Please.

I hope your *mea culpa* makes you feel better.

But listen.

The damage—whether slight, severe, or anywhere
        between—cannot be undone.

Your sincerity can be ever so genuine.

But the damage cannot be undone.

Apologizing for mistakenly stepping on my foot does not
        lessen the pain, remove the scuff on the shoe, or
        repair the ruined hose.

The same is true with the damage resulting from your
        carelessness, recklessness, meanness, confession, or
        plain ignorance.

Apologies may, indeed, make the guilty feel better, but the
        injured party—not necessarily.

Therefore, as much as is possible, live so as to avoid the
        need to make apologies.

03/09/06

The Inadequacy of Apologies

Spock did it.

Nobel did it.

Oppenheimer did it.

Flaky parents do it.

Deadbeat moms and dads do it.

Ungrateful kids do it.

Arrested speeders do it.

Drunk drivers are always doing it.

Criminals do it in court countless times everyday.

Governments do it.

Bush does it to the parents of dead soldiers.

What did or do all of these folks do?

Apologize.

Look. Apologizing for mistakenly stepping on my foot does
       not lessen the pain, remove the scuff on my shoe, or
       repair my ruined hose.

The same is always true with the damage resulting from
       carelessness, recklessness, meanness, confession, or
       plain ignorance.

Therefore, as much as is possible, live so as to avoid the
       need to make apologies.

03/09/06

For Your Information:
What You Ought to Know About Rules

Rules change.

The rules change.

The rules have changed.

The rules are changing.

The rules will change.

Who changes rules?

Foes, friends, and folks we don't know change rules.

Sometimes we ourselves change rules.

Whatever: we ought always recognize simple facts.

Always remember: rules change.

09/23/01

DECLARATIONS

Abandoned

Abandon.

Abandoned.

Abandonment.

We children never get past it.

Regardless of the reason:

We were just kids. (**You didn't know you were just kids?**)

We were immature. (**You didn't know you were immature?**)

My family was embarrassed. (**You had no idea they would be?**)

We wanted to finish school? (**You didn't before my conception?**)

He was married. (**When did you make this discovery?**)

We weren't right for each other? (**Sex can make you right for each other?**)

I had a scholarship. (**Now when did you get this scholarship?**)

It was just an overnight stand. (**All the more reason NOT to conceive!**)

We knew they could give you a better home. (**But THEY did not conceive!**)

We knew they could give you a better life. (**But THEY did not conceive me!**)

My family would never have accepted you. (**They accepted YOU before?**)

We didn't mean anything to each other. (**You meant enough to conceive a child?**)

I was at a point in my career.... (**You were not at this point when …..**)

I was not fit because of ….(**And you were fit when?**)

He/she never wanted children. (**He/she did want**
children BEFORE I was conceived?)

Regardless of your reason, we always have this void,
      sometimes very big, sometimes very small.

But we always have it, always know something's missing.

The void is there/here.

We realize that you yourself have had your problems—
      myriad problems.

You may be as wounded, more wounded than we are.

Your loving us, thinking about us, having us—like Willie
      Nelson—always on your mind may be good, but it's not
      something we know because we don't know your thoughts.

Your "I'm sorry," "I made a mistake," "I did a bad thing," "I
      accept responsibility" changes very little if anything.

Regardless of our gratitude to the people who altered their
      lives when we arrived—willingly or unwillingly—we
      were abandoned.

Many of us forgive you.

Many of us do not hate you.

We may not love you, but some of us do love you.

We understand you believe you did the best you knew how
      at the time with what you had.

And, dear parent, so did we, so do we.

06/13/04

Al Green Is Roping

Al Green is roping.
Al Green is always roping.
Tired of Being Alone
Call Me.
Love and Happiness
Living for You
Let's Stay Together.
Yes, Al Green is always roping.

The title comes from a line in
David Lindsay-Abaire's drama *Rabbit Hole.*
The next poem also refers to the play.

06/17/07

Both Grieved

He wants to talk; she doesn't.

He wants to keep the clothes; she doesn't.

He wants to keep the dog; she doesn't.

He wants to keep the toys; she doesn't.

He wants to ignore the driver; she doesn't.

He wants to listen to Al Green; she doesn't.

He wants to have sex; she doesn't.

He wants God's help; she doesn't.

He wants counseling; she doesn't.

He wants to keep the house; she doesn't.

He wants to change nothing; she wants to change everything.

Both felt guilty.

Both said neither was to blame; nobody was to blame.

Both grieved.

Both loved the child, missed the child.

They divorced each other every way but formally.

Grief can bury you in an Alice rabbit hole.

Grief can wipe out everything but the pain of the loss.

06/17/07

Breakdowns

There are two kinds of breakdowns: the rational and the
      irrational.

The irrational is the more common.

Someone looks at a situation, attacks the speaker rather
      than what the speaker says, uses deceptive statistics,
      makes a false analogy, evades the issue, begs the
      question, presents a false dilemma, succumbs to the
      old bandwagon rule everybody does it,
        Succumbs to these and more fallacies common to any
      elementary debater.

The irrational totals the so-called facts and concludes that
      escape is the answer.

After a war of great magnitude, for instance, the some who
      feel deeply choose to do battle no longer.

But there is no physical place to go because the mind goes
      wherever its owner goes.

The rational breakdown, however, has at its center the one
      who takes a toll and reasons "I can go no further."

This person knows "much madness is divinest sense and
      much sense, the starkest madness."

Madness is indeed nothing but "the nobility of the soul at
      odds with circumstances."

Yes, there are indeed rational breakdowns.

The question is how many of these breakdowns we must
      endure—"we" because we are in this together.

For both the breakdown of the rational and the irrational
        have the power to obliterate those of us who walk
        among them, those of us who valiantly struggle
        to maintain our sanity as we attempt to avoid the
        breakdowns of either kind.

Thanks to Theodore Roethke, Emily Dickinson,
Ernest Hemingway, and Ronald Hall

08/27/03

Choosing to Stay; Choosing to Go

Sometimes I stay because I am strong.

I examine the facts, hear the opposition, weigh both sides.

Then I draw my conclusion.

Staying means I accept what is—for now;

I will or cannot change what is—now.

I may not like it, but I choose to stay in the situation.

Maybe the situation will get better; maybe it won't.

But I will stay….

For now.

Sometimes I stay because I'm weak.

I examine the facts, hear the opposition, weigh both sides.

Then I draw my conclusion.

Staying means I accept what is—for now; I will or cannot
        change what is—for now.

I do not like the situation, but I choose to stay in the
        situation.

I will not fight.

Fighting requires energy and resolve, neither of which I
        have for this situation.

I choose to exert my energy on another front.

So I will stay.

Sometimes I go because I am weak.

Going means I reject what is; I will not or cannot accept
        what is.

I don't like the situation, so I choose to leave it.

Maybe the situation will get better; maybe it won't.

But I will not stay.

No amount of persuasion can convince me otherwise.

Sometimes I go because I am strong.

Surprisingly, I follow the same process as I do when I

        choose to stay.

Only I have the wherewithal to escape the situation.

Maybe the situation will change; maybe it won't.

However, neither matters.

Now, I choose to protest or battle.

The feeling is better when I go as a result of strength.

But so often I go because of weakness.

Going means I reject what is.

I may not like what is, may not want what is,

But reason says the best move is a move.

Sometimes I leave although I think I'm staying.

Other times I stay although I think I'm leaving.

Going and leaving, I've learned, often have little to do with

        distance.

But they constitute life, the life of the mind.

10/12/04

The Contractor

Contractor: that's what they called him,

Him and anyone else willing go to Iraq to rebuild what
Saddam and the U. S. tore down.

What got his attention was $4,000 per month, possibly
more, tax-free.

He made about half that at home where he is somewhat
safer.

$4,000 got him.

He signed up; he would be rich.

This would be a trip of a lifetime.

Six months later he's back home,
home from the longest six months of his life.

$24,000 richer financially,

But impoverished immeasurably.

He's been diagnosed with post-traumatic stress syndrome.

Mind you—he was not a mercenary; he didn't go to fight.

He certainly did not go to be shot at.

Shortly after his arrival, uneasiness took over.

He learned the meaning of risk.

He learned the meaning of fear.

On top of this were little problems: heat, dust, rain.

He'll tell you what many knew before his departure:
"It ain't worth it."

05/09-10/04

Days

There are days when I feel I've been fenced in, plowed
      under, hung out, raked over, displaced, or
      abandoned;
Days when everything is black or white;
Days when filters are intentionally applied.
I think, what's the use.
Of what use am I?
Why am I here?
Then I remind myself that so often only the good gets
      fenced in, plowed under, hung out, raked over,
      displaced, or abandoned.
I remind myself that I have been of value, am of value, will
      be of value.
And the wayward feeling passes because I am fertile and
      productive.
The world, at least my part of it, needs me to make my
      observations and express those observations
      however and whenever I can.
I have to help others be productive and fertile.
Plato was right: I am doomed to return to the cave, to
      return repeatedly and help all others escape as
      soon as possible, teach them that being responsible
      means risking all to save many, any.
This realization strengthens.
The day of the final fencing, plowing, hanging, raking,
      displacing, and abandoning is most certainly
      coming—but not today!

Inspired by John Martinotti's photographs   *08/04-06/04*

Escaping Thought

Escaping thought is not easy for me.

But there are those times when I escape.

I immerse myself in a book.

I see a play which speaks to me.

I dance the night away.

I teach people who want to be taught.

I drive around Mount Rainier or see Skagit Valley tulips.

I succumb to the desires of a grand niece or nephew.

I listen to a song, lecture, or sermon which teaches me or
       reminds me of something I learned.

I communicate genuinely.

Absolutely nothing is better than escaping thought but
       living the moment the thought is reality.

04/11/07

Homemade Dresses

Twenty-five pounds of flour or meal.

Who cares?

Let the girls see the sacks, the 100% cotton sacks.

They want this bag!

No, they'll take that one!

There's one at home that matches.

All eyes were involved in the selection.

The dexterous hands of an amazing mother could design,
        layout, cut, sew, press, and fit four dresses for four
        girls at an unimaginable speed.

Always for the first day of school, Easter and Christmas,
        any special occasion in between.

How were the girls they to know the love embedded in the dresses
        can never ever be found in a store-bought dress
        regardless of the price?

No one could have explained to their little minds and
        hearts that her love was in the details.

Now that the girls are women, the priceless acts are clearer
        than any act could ever have been in those days.

The women know there can't be a heaven unless the
        mother knows how grateful they are for the long-
        gone homemade dresses.

09/17/2002

Just Do It!

When Nike says, "Just do it," there's space to insert any
      noun for the "it."
Baseball, football, cycling, track, jogging, and any of many
      sports you can find at the Olympics and playfields all
      over the world.
And Nike just does it.
It makes shoes for any sport for which we need shoes.
It convinced us that we have to have a different shoe for
      each sport.
Then it convinced us we need a shoe to cross train.
No doubt about it, Nike just does it.

But for the people—usually women—who work in the
      factories, work is the word they always insert for "it."
Work is what they just do.
And do and do and do.
And working is the difference between starving and
      eating—for them and their families.
So while some—with the best of intentions—tell Nike to
      shut the shops, others say bring on the shops.
Because eating is almost always preferable to not eating,
      especially for those whom eating is not something they just do.

07/17/04

Just One, Only One

One word
One sentence
One assignment
One prank
One visit
One absence
One experiment
One hitchhiking excursion
One question
One answer
One pill
One drink
One final date
One fling
One night of wild sex
One time of saying "Let's get naked"
One time of not using birth control
One last-minute trick
One dose of Rohypnol
One tablet of ecstasy
One one-night stand
One spin of the trigger
One curve taken too fast
One grenade slipping from fingers

So often all it takes is one incident or event which
significantly divides our lives in two—a before and after.

11/18/03

Painters and Poets

Painters see lines, curves, colors, and space, even negative space.

Poets see words, words, words.

Painters see lines and curves others don't see.

Poets make others see.

Poets use pens to paint with words.

Painters use pens and brushes to write with paint.

Poets love verbs and adjectives and adverbs; they have to
       have nouns and pronouns too.

Painters never see a subject that can't be painted with the right medium.

Poets never hear a subject that can't be poem matter.

Join the painter and poet and inevitably you get a feast of sight and sound.

06/23/04

Lady and the Dog and the Missing Mates

A dog can be a woman's best friend.
It may not give much as some mates, but then it takes less,
       requires less than many mates.
And a ceramic dog, not to mention a drawn dog, requires
       less still!
This dog can see everything and see nothing.
The lady's not alone in wanting such a person some of the
       time.
Too often this mate sees nothing where the lady sees
       everything or everything where the lady sees nothing.
Yet she longs for a person who, like the dog, can strike a
       pose and not pose.
No posturers necessary, says she.
The dog is right there whether the mood is gold, red, black,
       or blue.
To have someone who sleeps when she sleeps, curls up
       when she curls up—anywhere and time she chooses
To curl in opposite directions without explaining,
       compromising, or apologizing.
No offense given or taken, says she.
To be alert when she's alert,
This dog makes no or few demands, demands which can
       be fulfilled without too much cost, space, time, or
       emotion.
Water, food, shelter, maybe a hug, a pat, a rub—none ever
       leading to entangling alliances, ulterior motives, ultimatums.

Mates, on the other hand, require so much more, especially
  those who treat the lady as she wishes to be treated
  and then, of course, as they wish to be treated.
And mates never wish to be treated like dogs,
  Though there are some dogs treated quite well.
The calm, serenity, tranquility devoutly wished so often
  comes so easily when the lady is with the dog.

02/01/05   Inspired by Karen Kosoglad's paintings

Let's Get Naked!

Let's get naked.
Well, maybe, but probably not.
There's a good chance couples who say "Let's get naked" are only shedding clothes.
But a couple who cares/loves/shares are naked,
Naked because they bared their minds and souls.
Their minds married.
They never had to or have to say, "Let's get naked."
They reveal who and what they are via speech and actions.
Their baggage serves as a steppingstone rather than a stumbling block.
They don't inflict pain because someone inflicted pain.
They alleviate all the pain they can.
They understand each other.
Of course, they don't always like the same things or do the same things.
But they appreciate each other's interest and involvement.
They are happiest when the other is happiest.
They never talk about this fifty-fifty stuff.
Each does 100% 100% of the time.
They really do get each other's jokes, even if no one else does.
They really do look across the room at each other at the same time.
When separated, they keep mental notes of what happens
         so they can share when they are together.

For them, absence really does make the heart grow fonder
         rather than yonder.
They know naked people may as well have their clothes on.
And they know that what they have is a rarity, a rarity some
         people never experience, worse, never know exists.

06/18/04

Lines and Curves

Does the pregnancy control the woman?

Or does the woman control the pregnancy?

Who is controlling whom?

It depends.

If the woman wants the baby—always Mama's baby—then
       the baby controls her.

Say the man tells her to get an abortion, never wanted
       a child, or her one and only partner says, "Get a
       paternity test."

Maybe her health is at risk.

To these and any other obstacle, she says, while ignoring
       the costs, "Be gone; this is my baby. I am having
       this baby."

On the other hand, if the woman does not want the fetus—
       an accident, mistake, inconvenience, unplanned—
       she controls it.

Say she has an important athletic event, won't tolerate the
       disfigurement.

Maybe she is up for a key move in her career.

Or she knows, or doubts, the fetus belongs to her husband
       or the man she loves, the man she's with.

To these and any other obstacle, she says, "Be gone; this is
       my body. I choose."

What we have is extreme sides of the same subject.

Both sides have their lines; both sides set their curves; both
       sides use their space.

Wanted—the subject has one meaning; unwanted—it has
    another.

Either way, the subject exists, leaves a mark.

This artist is silent, confesses to giving us only lines and
    curves and space.

But actually she gives us the space to define our lines and
    curves....

05/21/04

Mad at God

He's mad at God.
Yes, and he is not alone.
Others know the feeling.
Somebody you love dies.
Somebody who's the nicest, kindest, gentlest person is dead.
And somebody who's the opposite—nasty, mean,
        despicable—is alive.
You dislike yourself for thinking such thoughts.
You don't wish anyone dead.
You just wish someone you loved were alive.
You tell yourself you're dreaming, the person can't be dead,
        not *that* person.
Then you tell yourself to get a grip or, worse, someone
        tells you to get a grip.
You wonder where's the justice, the fairness.
How can this person be gone since God loves you?
God loved that person.
If someone had told you that you could live without this
        person, you would have declared you couldn't.
You look at the spouse, especially a mom or dad, the
        siblings, nieces, nephews, grandnieces and
        grandnephews.
You sometimes see the deceased in the features, actions,
        reactions, gestures of the descendants, of yourself.
You laugh when you realize you look, act as this person did.
You surprise yourself by saying what this person said.
Times you aren't thinking about the deceased you see
        something which reminds you, makes you recall, remember.

Sometimes you smile; other times you laugh.

And there are those times you cry, a secret cry.

Sometimes you feel so much better after telling someone
your thoughts.

Sometimes this person has to be someone who knew the
deceased.

Other times you tell someone whom you don't know,
especially someone you meet on an airplane.

And countless times you say you've got to stop this, you've
got to get past this, over this.

You tell yourself other people move on, people you know
loved this person have moved on, you think.

And then you say but our relationship was different.

And then you hear one more person use that word
"closure."

And you go crazy because you know you'll never have that.

There are days you feel it just happened.

There are days you remember all of those well-meaning
words people say the first time they see you after the
death: "If there's something I can do…."

And despite your grief, you know you can't scream, "Yes,
bring her back!"

Sometimes you think they know there is nothing they can
do, but they have to say, "Let me know if there is
something I can do."

And you play along, knowing there is nothing they can do.

On your worst days you say they know there is nothing they
can do.

And then there are those other little sentences--all
　　　　declarative:
"He is in a better place."
"She won't suffer anymore."
"God knows best."
"This was God's will."
"You'll see her again one day—just be good."
"He was tired."
"She lived a good life."
"He lived a long life."
And you realize "I'm sorry" is probably the best one
　　　　although it, like the others, does not work, does not
　　　　ease the pain.
No words ease the pain although everybody really
　　　　does mean well.
For the first time you really know what Ray Charles means
　　　　when he says, "Time has stood still since we've been
　　　　apart."
Oh, you're mad with God.
And though it may take you a while—months, years,
　　　　decades—maybe, just maybe, one day—because you have to know
　　　　God to be mad with God—you'll come to realize God
　　　　knows.
God knows, and God cares.
And, most of all, God is alive.

05/26-27/04

The List

I found a list,

Almost fifty names on it.

Don't know when I wrote it.

Don't know what it was for, when it was made.

There are lines through the names.

So I must have accomplished the tasks.

By your name is the figure two,

The only name so marked.

But that's the way it is with me when you're on the list.

And you're always on the list: call, e-mail, tell, ask, send,
        thank.

You're at least twice as important as anyone else.

I care so much.

I always want to please you so much.

I always want you to have what you need and want.

I never want you to be hurt.

That's so much for one little person to want for a person as
        big as you.

Yet that's the only way I know how to be.

So I'll keep making lists.

06/18/04

Markers

Dates of birth and dates of death often line tombstones.
But a smart person somewhere has said "It is the dash
      placed between the dates that counts."
What counts gets markers.
And all of the markers are not disasters.
We mark birthdays.
We mark the first day of school.
We mark graduations.
We mark marriages.
And then we start the process again.
The markers are not equal.
Everybody does not get all of the markers, and all of the
      markers do not get equal attention.
The Day the Japanese bombed Pearl Harbor and the Day
      Roosevelt died—that's Ann.
The Day World War II ended—that's Dad.
The Day Mama died—that's M'Dear.
The Day Kennedy was shot, killed—that's for everyone in
      the country who was over ten in '63.
9/11....
We need markers.
They may remind us of what to do and what not to do.
They may give us the strength to make our dreams—
      including the wildest ones—realities.

They may convince us that our freakish impulses can be

      realized and without harm or danger.

They may provide the focus to tread forward regardless of the price.

Sometimes they may tell us to return to get wisdom, knowledge, to help someone.

Sometimes markers may simply light the path.

Inspired by art of David Traylor and Cindy Hall   *09/03/03*

No Baby, No Way – at Least Not Tonight

Fifteen when she married,
Married a man twelve years her senior.
She hadn't had any say in the decision to marry.
She had less say in the marriage.
Husband decided when to have sex.
Never made love to her.
Baby one arrives; she's not quite sure how.
She worked from before sunup to beyond sundown.
He owned her like he owned the ground.
Both were fertile.
Both were ploughed.
Both produced.
Both giving, giving, giving, and giving some more.
Never having a say.
Being sowed.
Sowing seeds.
Having babies.
Harvesting crops.
Just as she cropped.
Collecting eggs.
Gathering children.
Sewing clothes.
Being sowed again.
Feeding chickens.
Feeding babies.
Slopping pigs.
Cleaning babies.
Pitching hay.

Combing hair.
Cutting wood.
Picking up babies.
Making bread.
Making babies.
Making beds.
Raising children.
Washing, ironing.
Burying a baby here and there.
Cooking, cooking oh so much cooking.
Another baby in her stomach oven.
Canning jellies.
Carrying babies.
Storing jams.
So one night when it was so late,
So late she knew he'd come home drunk,
She decided there would be no baby tonight.
She left the house, hid in the woods cold and wet.
Cold and wet, she hid.
Hadn't known how cold it could get so late at night,
Hadn't thought about the wet of the woods.
Wanted to escape the wet on and in her body.
So she was safe, safe from another baby.
Cold and wet but safe.

Finally he came,
Drunk as ever,
Drunk as expected.

Reeling, he stumbled in the yard,
Fell a few more times.
But soon, soon he missed her,
Not too drunk to know she wasn't there.
Called her—slurred her name,
Just as he had spoiled her.
Called some more,
All the while ranting when he could get a word out.
Still seeking her body.
Never knew she had a soul.
The alcohol wins.
Sleep comes.

When she doesn't hear him, she too sleeps.
Happy there is no baby.
Satisfied that there is no baby.
She knew there would be a price for this obvious defiance.
But the young woman had no way of knowing what that price would be.
She knew she had to prepare breakfast and do all the other
        chores her young body had become accustomed to
        or as well as one could become accustomed to....
Early the next morning she slips into the house.
He's sprawled on the floor—
Where he almost made it to the bed.
He sleeps.

She gets babies up, dressed, and fed.
It seemed he'd sleep forever.
She went about her countless chores.
Still not thinking about what would happen
Only thinking about no baby.

But, of course, he awakened.
By now she was hanging laundry on the line, in the sun.
She had no idea he had been watching her.
Now he slowly and crookedly stumbles and half falls down the steps.
She hears him,
Gets afraid for the first time today.
He does not approach her,
Rather he goes toward a prop holding up the clothesline
She who never had a prop
Turns to see him approaching her
Approaching with that prop from the line.
Startled, she stands,
Seeing what's coming and yet not seeing what's coming.
Not watching her not knowing what to try to protect,
He slammed that prop against that little woman, knocking her down.
Woman only because Mom always said, "You aren't a
                woman 'till you have a baby."
She crumpled in the fetal position,
Managing to let out a scream.
He hit her until she could make no attempt to escape his licks.
He pounded her with the prop.
A prop meant to hold up was beating down.

But not before he and the prop had pounded her down.

The drunkenness saved her.

Though strong, he was not as strong as the undrunk man was.

He pounded until he himself fell.

Hours later when she awakened, she vaguely remembered what happened.

She knew she was wounded, bloody, swollen.

But most of all, she knew there would be no baby.

Her joy lasted only momentarily because she had to start

      planning to keep him away again.

She knew he would not sleep forever.

Her only comfort was knowing inside her was no baby,

      Not tonight.

03/20/04

Our Rights Are in Danger

Our rights are in danger.

I have known this for such a long time.

Yet, I see newspaper and magazine articles and read
> e-mails about our rights and how we are losing them.

What I want to say is simple: one must have rights before
> those rights can be endangered.

I am the result of a long line of people whose rights were
> non-existent despite the beautiful language in the
> Declaration of Independence and the Constitution.

Clearly, I have a history of having rights not only being in
> danger but not being enforced or exercised.

Do you want to talk about bombed churches?

Or do you prefer unreasonable searches?

You could talk about all of those lynching "convictions" minus a trial.

As for a "jury of peers" and a "speedy trial" or excessive bail, we need
> a jury first.

We know about justice delayed.

Once again, we have people screaming why they are
> "threatened."

Where were they when for so long nobody acknowledged
> my rights and the rights of so many others?

How long will it take for us to realize the truth of the
> statement "Our rights are in danger"?

I know the answer to my question: when we realize
> endangering the rights of one endangers the rights of all,
> then we will know just how much our rights are in danger.

2004

Precious Cargo

The Pentagon has a policy of not showing coffins—respect
    for and dignity of the dead.
The photographer took the picture of coffins because she was awed
    by the workers' respect for and dignity extended the dead.
Is there a problem?
Pentagon and photographer saw the same but interpreted what
    they saw differently.
During Viet Nam NBC showed troops happily arriving home.
In the background of the same frames NBC
    showed troops solemnly departing for Viet Nam.
Someone said we would want to stop the war when people
    began returning in body bags.
Actually, some of us did not want the war to begin.
Please let me explain: some of us did not want the war to begin.
We did not want to see body bags; we did not want to see them ever again.
We never wanted there to be body bags.
Cargo is not cargo.
Some cargo is different.
Yet how respectful caretakers are does not change the state of the cargo.
Whether enemy soldier, guerilla or friendly fire, on or off
    the field, hand or rocket-propelled grenade, an I. E. D.,
    combat, suicide, auto crash, or any of the
    many ways men have devised to kill "the other" and
    one another: the cargo is dead, carefully handled
    although the living being may have been handled so carelessly in life.
The red, white, and blue flags are draped neatly.
We are told the flags are draped carefully.
Not one coffin atop another coffin.

(Imagine how much space and fuel could be saved if they
        really filled the planes!)
But no expense is too high an expense for our dead.
Carefully handled and neatly contained yet still dead.
The living, of course, is another story.
Dead.
Dead.
Photographs of such cargo from other countries may be
        handled equally as well.
After all, those countries' precious cargo is equally dead.
At least Iraqi dead die at home, but they are no less precious.
Maybe flags of red, white, black, and green drape their bodies.
All dead.
Dead.
Dead.
What is so hard about understanding that some of us want no more dead,
        that some of us see killing in retaliation for killing just
        equals an increase in the number dead?
This world has seen enough precious cargo; we've seen it
        even when the government has decreed not to photograph it.

04/21/04

Real Words

Here my friends are some "real words,"
Not a forwarded e-mail labeled "good" or "beautiful" or
       "inspirational" or even the ubiquitous often misused
       "awesome."
Here are real words from me to you.
I wish you health, good health—mental and physical—
       regardless of your age.
I want you to be pain-free, even those pains some call
       "peculiar to your age."
When you don't move, I want it to be because you don't
       want to, never because you can't.
I wish you family, friends, folks who know and love you as
       you are,
Folks who trust you even when they disagree with you,
Folks around whom you can lose your temper without
       losing them,
Folks whom you may contact irregularly but always
       genuinely.
I wish that although you may be alone, you'll never be
       lonely.
I wish you the wherewithal to live at least as you're
       accustomed and better if you can.
I want you to have all the necessities, of course, but
       so much that you never have to worry that they will
       be removed.
And most of all, I wish you the faith to know the love and
       security that come only from the Highest Power.

02/03/05

Relics

Displaced wheels

Plowed-out fields

Fenced-in fields

Hung-up hats

Forgotten equipment

Raked fields

Abandoned chairs

Old barns, lanterns, saws, bottles....

What do these items have in common?

All have had their time.

Everything has its time, its season.

Though we may not have known the "thing" in its heyday,

      the "thing" served its purpose.

The photographs are great testimonies.

Although the seasons vary, each item in its time plays its

      part.

Maybe the relics are here to remind us that at least one of

      the above words will indeed be used to describe us.

They may describe us.

But maybe they warn us to get a move on.

Inspired by John Martinotti's photographs.   *08/03/04*

Still Lifes

No clock or candles or hour-glasses
No empty containers—cup, bowl, or pitcher
No crown, scepter, jewel, purse, coins
No weapons
No skulls
No peelings
Just flowers, cut flowers
Flowers which were living but were cut
So, while living they were alive; they were not still life
But after being cut, they are labeled still life.
Beautiful, we say.
Proof God exists, some say.
Cut flowers are not disturbing, not sad
But the cut flowers are, indeed, dead.

Maybe we like them so much because cut flowers are like us.
We have our being and we move.
And simultaneously we're enroute to the fate of the flowers,
Shakespeare put it another way: we ripe and ripe and then we rot and rot,
A fate which began not on our birthday but rather at conception.
Somehow cut flowers don't always remind us that they're dead even as we
     discard them.
They don't remind us we're dying.
No—the still lifes stop life at a most beautiful moment,
And some of us love this moment, lovingly cling to this moment.
Cut flowers—especially painted ones, give us memorable moments.

2004   Inspired by Pamela Mills' painting *Offering (9) Sunflowers on Blue*

Time Was and Time Is

From B.C. to A. D.

Before and After

Then and Now

Sleeping to Waking

Eyes Wide Shut to Eyes Wide Open

Deaf to Hearing

Numb to Feeling

Why, the sighted Oedipus never sees what blind Oedipus sees

Just as the sighted Gloucester never sees what the blind Gloucester sees

Or, most miraculously, the sane Lear never knows what the mad Lear knows.

Our lives are punctuated by revelations and epiphanies

     which the world usually doesn't notice: the world is .

     not seeing, hearing, smelling, touching, or tasting.

Nevertheless, we take notice, never again to see, hear,

     smell, touch, or taste—alas, to be—the same.

2004

War and Fair

Fair.

Fair, people.

All is fair in war.

All is fair in war, people.

What makes decapitating worse than bombing?

Is it the up close, personal killing of the one versus the aim,
       fire, killing of the many?

Is it the immediate certain death of the one versus the
       eventual certain deaths of the many?

Fear and restriction are present before and after the killing
       as are impotence and loss.

War.

It's war, people.

In war, everybody loses.

And, yes, somebody loses less or more.

That's as close as I can come to fair: everybody loses.

2004

What My Silence Means

Don't misread my silence.

It doesn't always mean consent.

There are times when it means dissent.

It may mean I'm scared, but maybe not.

It could mean I'm sad.

I could be sulking, meditating, hurting.

Maybe my silence is giving birth to the mother of silences.

Maybe I'm contemplating, thinking.

But maybe, just maybe, I'm silently perfecting a strategy to
        unleash the ocean within.

It is easier to misread my silence than read it right.

So, please be careful.

Don't misread my silence.

10/09/04

Why Some of Us Holler

You are looking at a healthy baby whom doctors told you
        could not be conceived.
Or, you're well forty-three years after the doctors told
        your mother you probably would not get to be six years old.
Or, you're out of jail twenty-seven years after knowing you
        were innocent—and you are not bitter.
Or, you're a Ph. D. after having begun college with only a five-dollar bill.

Some of us who holler know for a fact God is in charge.
Talk to any sane person no longer the least, lost, locked up, or left out.
Maybe then you can understand why some of us holler.
Hollering is not something planned.
Hollering happens.
We holler because we know humans are not ultimately in charge.
We holler because we know God is.

03/27/08

Power People

I wonder what presidents, premiers, prime ministers, and
      kings say when officials tell them there's a casualty
      in war.
Do they say, "Damn," "Shucks," "Wow," or "I never
      expected this?"
Do they curse or bow their heads or say a prayer?
Do they ask some Superior Being, "Why"?
Do they think about the moms and dads, sisters and
      brothers, sons and daughters, aunts and uncles,
      wives and husbands, cousins and friends?
Do they think about the voids created because of the
      departures?

Me? Oh, I never want anybody to go to war.
Oh, I always think communication can solve the problem.
That's genuine, as in honest, communication.
I won't argue about the wars before my coming, especially
      the one they said would end all wars.
But since I have been here, I don't think there has been a
      war that had to be.
In all of them there is fighting, killing, and then signing a
      treaty,
I say let's fast forward and skip the killing.
Let's talk.
See, I pray the moms and dads, sisters and brothers,
      sons and daughters, aunts and uncles, wives and
      husbands, cousins and friends will be ok.

But I know they nor the returning soldiers will never be the
        ok they were before the soldiers went.
There are the dead about whom we can do nothing but
        express condolences and give a sum of money.
There are the physically maimed for whom we can pay
        medical bills.
There are the mentally ill for whom we MAY pay medical
        bills but often send on their way only to read
        their obituaries after they have killed someone or
        ones and themselves.
And then there are all of those who have no visible scars.
We don't keep track of them or the changes—the broken
        relationships, nightmares.
This madness is much too much.
It can drive a sane person mad.

I wish I didn't wonder what the presidents, premiers, prime
        ministers, and kings say when officials tell them
        there's a casualty in war.

02/27/03

A Primal Truth

This forty-two year-old woman told me she was thirty-six
>   when she learned everybody did not love her....

I wondered where she had been.

I have known at least since I was eight that everybody did/does not love me.

I am so glad she has parents who loved her dearly–and showed it.

I wonder did she have siblings.

Not one classmate hated her?

My experiences are replete with folks who not only not
>   loved me or somebody else but excluded me or somebody
>   else because someone decided what counts.

It must be so amazing to live four decades believing everyone loves you!

Some slave masters said they were saving Africans: how else
>   could Africans have known about the God of the English Bible?

What is ethnic cleansing—whether in Germany or Chechnya—
>   but the destruction of the "inferior" as defined by the oppressor?

But today a young woman sees Shakespeare's shrew is as blond as
>   she is rather than the bad, dark-haired person some paint her to be.

Somebody else is so thrilled to see a black Mark Antony, a black Juliet.

These choices are made because of notions, concepts,
>   conclusions which may have absolutely nothing to
>   do with truth and possibly everything to do with hate.

Hate of color, creed, culture, size, intelligence—you name it.

If you were hated before age thirty-six, you can name a few so-called reasons.

To have had the freedom which must come with believing
>   everyone loves you, to have had it four decades...

To live to be forty-two before discovering the primal truth
       everybody does not love me might have empowered
       me to soar to unspeakable heights.
But then this truth might have landed me in a place from
       which she had just been released.

02/27/03

When Sunday Comes...

When Sunday comes, I'm not thinking about Monday when
a love disappeared or someone misunderstood
I'm not thinking about Tuesday when the washer and the disposer stopped and
the meeting went all wrong
I'm not thinking about Wednesday when a friend lost a valiant battle with
cancer and another was diagnosed with the dreaded
disease.
The Thursday car accident does not cross my mind.
I'm not thinking about the Friday death count revelation in Iraq ....
I'm not thinking about the aches and pain from all of Saturday's gardening.

No, when Sunday comes, I'm thinking The Lord is in His
holy temple, faith is the substance of things hoped for, wait on the Lord.
When Sunday comes, I'm thinking God loves me.
I see His love in the faces, glances, nods, and smiles of
worshippers.
I feel Him in the touches and hugs and kisses.
I hear Him in songs and sermons that remind me He is and
I love to praise Him.
When Sunday comes, I get what I need to do what needs to
be done Monday through Saturday and sometimes
Sunday ....
Hallelujah!
I'm always glad when Sunday comes!

09/22/04

Wearing My Mother's Face

I don't know when I began wearing my mother's face.
Other folks recognized I was wearing my mother's face
        before I did.
They told me.
I'd smile and keep going.
Nieces and nephews thought pictures of my mother were
        pictures of me.
I'd smile and keep going.
Then one day I realized I was wearing my mother's face.
I smile more and keep going.

06/15/07

Dawn Dance

If I were a praise dancer,
I'd twirl and twist and turn.
I'd never miss a beat.
I'd stomp and step.
I'd bend, extend.
I'd jump high.
I'd squat low.
I'd strain, stretch my hands toward the sky.
I'd be happy, grateful, and blessed, the proof in each
    muscle.
I'd find a garment of the brightest colors, a garment of
    fabric that moved as gracefully as I.
I'd dance at dawn, my favorite time.
I'd dance on the beach, my favorite place.
I'd need no audience, just sun and sky, and the slightly
    moist sand beneath my feet.
I'd have no doubts.
I'd be so free, so focused.
I'd hear my Creator say, "Well done."

08/14/08

Seeing Toys

"I want to see all the toys!" screeched the little boy.

I knew immediately that he was not alone.

I want to see all the toys.

Many toys require only a glance.

Some I care not to touch.

But there are other toys for which a touch is insufficient.

These toys demand examination.

They beg me to pick them up, look closely and carefully.

I have to see what they can do, consider doing it myself.

I want to see all the toys so I can know what to do with
        which, how many suit my fancy.

But like the little boy whose Dad had scooped him up and
        taken him away, I can't see all the toys.

All I can do is look at the toys with which I come in contact.

Something or someone is always dragging me away or
        blocking my view, telling me there's no time to play
        or I'm too big to play.

I never tell anyone I want to see all the toys.

But I take and make time to see as many as I can as often as
        I can.

06/18/07

We All Want Something

We all want something.

     A nod

     A smile

     A yes

     A no

     A thank you

     Support

     Respect

     Sex

     Money

     Wealth

     Health

     Attention

     Recognition

Acknowledgement

This is neither good nor bad but a fact plain and simple:

Regardless of what is said, we all want something.

02/09

No Help

I want to say

> His death is God's will.
>
> He's done what all of us have to do.
>
> He's in a better place.
>
> He's pain-free.
>
> He was tired.
>
> He needed rest.
>
> He was ready.
>
> He had a good life.
>
> He lived a full life.
>
> He made space for someone else.

I usually believe all of the above.

But not one nor any combination reduces my pain.

Not one nor any combination makes me miss him less.

Call it selfishness.

I call it honesty: I want him here.

06/07/07

If Only

If only I had asked for less,
not wanted the best,
been satisfied to survive,
never known I could live and thrive,
taken the line of least resistance,
settled for anything,
accepted everything,
Then life would have been conflict-free.
Because there would be no me!

04/25/06

What You See

My neighbor asked where I'd been the past few days.
New York, I said, with the same exuberance that emerges
       whenever I talk about New York!
"New York!" said she in disdain.
Almost disregarding her response, I said, Yes, I love New York!
"How can you love New York? There is so much garbage."
I love the skyscrapers, theaters, subways, people, library,
       Metropolitan Museum….
"But what about the garbage?"
Oh, the history: Harlem, Abyssinian Baptist Church, St. Patrick's
       Cathedral, Riverside….
(I tried hard: I could not remember any garbage!)
"All I saw was garbage," she said, "on every corner, piled
       to the side of the streets."
But the Statue, the bridges, the lights, the water,
       Central Park, The Towers….
''No, all I saw was the garbage."
I smiled a smile not akin to the one I had at the beginning
       of the conversation.
But the next time I went to New York, I looked for garbage.
AND I FOUND IT.

1999

Two for One

Two toothbrushes
Two deodorants
Two beds
Two alarm clocks
Two VCR's
Two Thanksgivings
She would have gladly relinquished one-half her belongings.
She would have settled for their loving each other one-half
       as much as each loved her.
She would have gladly given up Dad's one house and Mom's one house.
All she ever wanted was two parents in one house, a house
       neither Mom's house nor Dad's house but rather our house.

Inspired by Elizabeth Halfacre's collage *Mom's House, Dad's House*   *2006*

Courses

Some courses aren't worth taking or staying.

Some battles aren't worth fighting.

Some prizes aren't worth winning.

At least they are not worth MY taking, staying, fighting, or winning.

Once I learned these truths, Life became easier to live, more enjoyable.

This knowledge is an example of power.

The freedom which comes from knowing, being aware...

The freedom of knowing I can choose to adapt, migrate, or disappear has

countless times kept me from dying.

08/06/04

Funerals – Not for Her

She did not come to Daddy's funeral.
Wishing Daughter had been there, Mama kept quiet.
Mama knew Daddy had not been the best of dads, hadn't been a good dad.
Shucks.
The only good said about him is he never left Mama and the kids.
And some would say that was bad: he should have left.
With no explanation, Daughter calmly said, "I am not coming."

Ten years later, Mama died.
Everybody was surprised when Daughter missed this funeral too.
No one doubted Daughter's love for Mama.
But Daughter refused to come to Mama's funeral.
Never said why.
Sent flowers, as if she were a friend of the family.

The family heard from mutual friends.
Daughter said Mama should never have had so many children.
Daughter said there was never time for her.
Daughter said she never got that attention all the books say children
        need to thrive.
Daughter said she was always looking after the younger children.
Daughter said she worked as hard as any woman, never had time to be a girl.

Poor baby.
Sixty years old.
Can't forget, won't forget, can't get over it.

The pain is still there, still there after all of these years.
The pain is as fresh as it was all those years ago.

Mommies and Daddies beware: The pain you cause—definitely deliberate or
      sadly unintentional—can permanently scar babies.
And being told that Mama—and Daddy even—did the best they could with what
      they had and what they knew is often little or no comfort.

2004

Good Time

I've had good time, wonderful time, fabulous time, more time than a great many.
Yet I want more time.
I need more time.

Time to see more sunrises and sunsets.
Time to see more streams, lakes, oceans, and seas.
Time to see more flowers and mountains, especially Rainier.

Time to see more siblings more often.
Time to see friends.
Time to see folks I don't know.

Time to see a play by Shakespeare, Williams, or Miller.
Time to hear Mama in *Raisin in the Sun* and Troy in *Fences*.
Time to hear the Inspirational Choir and Cookie, Susie, Starla, Venice, Charles,
    Cherie, and Phyllis.
Time to hear Pacino, Hoffman, DeNiro, Denzel Washington, and James Earl Jones say
    anything but a commercial.

Time to read another book, see another movie.
Time to write more.

Time to hear a sermon that makes me believe all over again.

Time to dance another night away.
Time to entertain and be entertained.

Time to eat more barbecue, boiled corn, potato salad, potato pie, collards, catfish, salad, gumbo, homemade ice cream, Louisiana watermelon, Szechwan or Thai anything.

I've had good time.
Yet I want more time.

11/19/04

The Modern Quilters

There's a diversity among quilters' fabrics that everyone can't see:
Cotton and cotton only
A combination of cotton plus whatever other fabric happens to be around
Or perhaps only a particular piece
Never used heirloom fabric
100 % remnants of precious garments having been worn by precious people
discoveries at a thrift store
no expense spared at a specialty boutique
gifts from folks who share and understand
goods from a shopping spree, perhaps.
There's a method in their crazy quilts:
a pattern meticulously plotted and executed
A mistake applied intentionally repeated
A specific color and its many shades and patterns
Two or three dimensions, blocks of every size
Not just time to think about a subject
But freedom to consider a theme, ponder an idea
Whimsical, serious, happy, sad
An imitation or original
Made leisurely over months or hurriedly over a week
All by oneself or with the help of friends
Machine pieced, hand stitched, or hand quilted
Speaking as boldly as any Miles, Bird, or Coltrane
But speaking not the same, not to everybody,
Not the same to the artist all the time each time
Blessing this one, comforting that one
Always a platform for sharing though not always sharing similarly.
The modern quilters leave valuables as vivid and honest as any ever left at any time.

Inspired by Pacific Northwest African-American Quilters   *03/19/09*

Not Always Possible

No!
Stop it!
Don't say it!
It is not true!
I don't care how sincere you are.
Your wealth and power mean little.

You can't always protect me.
You can't always be there for me.
You can't always be here for me.
I wish you could.

But thanks for wanting to protect me.
Thanks for trying to protect me.
Just knowing you want to, that you'll try to, makes everything easier.

02/24/06

What Really Claimed Carla

Cotton claimed Carla, she confessed.

The bed's a desk or table; no need to make it.

Adrenaline can take care of sleep.

No one has to eat everyday!

Dishes don't have to be done.

Dust can keep.

Sweeping, mopping, vacuuming—not now; they get done all the time.

Skip the exercise class—a day or two.

Return calls later.

Bills don't have to be paid today.

Postpone the errands.

Shopping can always wait.

The closet is full of clothes.

No one is visiting today.

The grass won't leave.

Finish the book tomorrow.

The play runs another week.

The report, the meeting—another time.

Something else is calling now.

And it is not cotton.

No, 'twas not cotton that called or claimed her.

'Twas art that pushed everything aside.

'Twas art and creativity that demanded a response.

There's no rest until the artist births the mind-occupying art.

I know.

I too am often claimed by art.

03/19/09

Directionless

I have no map, no recipe, no blueprints.

There is no rehearsal.

There is no dry run.

There is no rough draft.

There is no mock-up.

Yet I have to move, alternately slow or fast, but usually somewhere in between.

Plod?

Amble?

Lurch?

Walk?

Run?

Move.

Says my friend regularly, "It's called life."

05/29/06

Lear Was a King

Lear was a king.

Thought he was a king,

Said he was a king,

Every inch a king.

But he really was a pawn.

Didn't know he was a pawn,

Never thought he was a pawn.

But a pawn he was,

Used to having pawns who fawned.

But he did not know the pawns fawned,

Different prices for different pawns.

A pawn king is a kingly pawn.

Played games with family and friends,

But too late discovered they were playing games with him.

Maybe he didn't know he was playing games with them.

"Tell me how much you love me."

How much of a game is that?

Love's not love....

The two daughters who said everything he wanted to hear gave
    him nothing—

Unless you want to call the hell he endured something.

The one daughter who said "nothing" gave everything,

Knew her sisters for what they were,

Knew the two sisters/daughters were playing a game.

Or is it three sisters/daughters playing a game?

Ok. So, they aren't playing the same game,

But the daughters and dad are playing games, nevertheless.

Maybe the daughters had to play games because they learned early Dad played games.

The king was most ignorant when he thought he was most wise.

Even one unwise daughter was wise enough to know the king had slenderly known himself.

So he was a fool when he had a fool.

And his fool knew the king was a fool.

The fool said he himself would not be the king.

The good earl knew the king was a fool,

Makes a fool of himself serving the king.

Equally foolish, the king's best friend never saw when he could see.

Yet he saw everything when he was blind.

This friend's sane son pretended to be mad.

The friend's bastard son was really a bastard.

But his bastardy had nothing to do with illegitimacy.

He pretended to be good.

He was a bad guy who knew the stars had nothing to do with his being bad.

But he told folks the stars had everything to do with who they were.

Then he laughed at those who believed the lies.

He duped his gullible brother and unfaithful dad, his faithful brother and gullible dad,

Both of whom were "basically" good but not wise—for a long while,

One blind, the other not—both able to see too late to help either very long.

Still the dad was wise enough to note we humans are as flies to wanton boys, killed for sport.

And his friend the pawn, whether sane or mad, sometimes made sane statements:

"Reason not the need," he said; if need is uppermost, then just about everything is superfluous.

Despite the hell, he said, "Forget and forgive."

He asked a question universal, a question the aggrieved beg to have answered even when unable to voice it as Poet Lear does: "Why should a dog, a horse, a cat have life, and [good] thou no breath at all?"

Yes, Lear was a king and a pawn.

He was a puppet and a pauper too.

Like all of us, he got to play many parts.

However, we who dare examine his travel can be winners because he lights the way.

Outside our caves we often see the foolishness, the madness.

But the sighted can also see bonds, fidelity, love.

Maybe, just maybe, our endgame can be different.

Inspired by Adam Korpak's cartoon   *06/18/04*
Just A Pawn in the Game (King Lear)

INDEX

About the Author

GEORGIA STEWART McDADE, a Louisiana native who has lived in Seattle more than half her life, loves reading and writing. As a youngster she wrote and produced plays for her siblings and neighbors and collaborated with church youth to write plays for special occasions. As a charter member of the African-American Writers' Alliance (AAWA), she began reading her stories in public in 1991. She credits AAWA with making her regularly write poetry. For a number of years she has written poems inspired by artists at such sites as Gallery 110, Seattle Art Museum, Columbia City Gallery, and Art/Not Terminal. Georgia writes for Pacific Newspapers, especially the *South District Journal*, and volunteers at community radio station KBCS (91.3 FM). Among her several writing projects are the biography of her high school principal, a collection of her short stories, and journals kept on her six-month, solo trip around the world.